YOUR TIME IS THE SEED OF YOUR LIFE

An ultimate collection of substantial quotes about time management, procrastination and laziness

ROBERT HENRIKAS

DEDICATION

"To all who strive for better time management. To all seeking harmony between work and play. To all seekers of productivity, efficiency and balance in their lives; this book is dedicated to you. Let it be a true companion on your journey in life leading you to a life of purpose and fulfillment, a life well-spent and well-lived."

Your Time is the Seed of Your Life

Robert Henrikas

TABLE OF CONTENTS

INTRODUCTION

 *Time management is the secret ingredient to a successful recipe for life."*

In the mayhem of our cutting edge modern lives, time has turned into an extremely valuable currency. We are continually searching for available resources to boost our efficiency, accomplish our objectives, dreams, and aspirations and capitalize on each valuable moments. In any case, notwithstanding our best expectations, we frequently fall into the pit of lingering sluggishness and procrastination that prevent our advancement and afterward leave us in a state of hopelessness.

This empirical assortment of existential quotations about time management, procrastination and laziness is intended to spur you and give you the weapons required to overcome hindrances on the road to success, thereby making a course for progress. From the smart considerations of scholars to the practical advices of popular visionaries to the empowerment of notorious leaders, thinkers and time management experts from all walks of life, this book carries you through the transformative secrets of productivity. As you flip through these pages, you will discover the secrets to increased productivity, increased confidence, and a renewed sense of purpose and excellence in achieving your dreams through efficient time management.

CHAPTER 1

TIME MANAGEMENT QUOTATIONS FROM

FAMOUS FIGURES

1."Time is what we want most, but what we use worst." *— William Penn*

2."Time management is life management." *— Robin Sharma*

3."The bad news is time flies. The good news is you're the pilot." *— Michael Altshuler*

4."Time is a created thing. To say 'I don't have time' is like saying, 'I don't want to.'" *— Lao Tzu*

5."Your future is created by what you do today, not tomorrow." — ***Robert Kiyosaki***

6."Don't count the days; make the days count." — ***Muhammad Ali***

7."You may delay, but time will not." — ***Benjamin Franklin***

8."Time is the most valuable coin in your life. You and you alone will determine how that coin will be spent." — ***Carl Sandburg***

9."Lost time is never found again." — ***Benjamin Franklin***

10."The shorter way to do many things is to only do one thing at a time." — *Mozart*

11."Time is a great healer, but a poor beautician." — *Lucille S. Harper*

12."Time is the wisest counselor of all." – *Pericles*

13."Time management is an oxymoron. Time is beyond our control, and the clock keeps ticking regardless of how we lead our lives. Priority management is the answer to maximizing the time we have." — *John C. Maxwell*

14. "Time is really the only capital that any human being has, and the only thing they can't afford to lose." — *Thomas Edison*

15. "The common man is not concerned about the passage of time, the man of talent is driven by it." – *Shoppenhauer*

16. "Time flies over us, but leaves its shadow behind." — *Nathaniel Hawthorne*

17. "Don't wait. The time will never be just right." — *Napoleon Hill*

18."Time is the most precious gift you can give to someone, as it's like giving a portion of your life that you can never get back." — ***Rick Warren***

19."A man who dares to waste one hour of time has not discovered the value of life." — ***Charles Darwin***

20."Until we can manage time, we can manage nothing else." — ***Peter Drucker***

21."Time is a created thing. Say 'yes' to it." — ***Miles Davis***

22."You cannot kill time without injuring eternity." — ***Henry David Thoreau***

23. "The more you engage with time management, the greater your capacity to lead your own life." — *Brian Tracy*

24. "Time management is about life management." — *Idowu Koyenikan*

25. "Lack of direction, not lack of time, is the problem. We all have twenty-four hour days." — *Zig Ziglar*

26. "Time is the coin of your life. It is the only coin you have, and only you can determine how it will be spent. Be careful lest you let other people spend it for you." — *Carl Sandburg*

27."One can find time for everything if one is never in a hurry." — *Mikhail Bulgakov*

28."Time is what keeps everything from happening at once." — *Ray Cummings*

29."The trouble is, you think you have time." – *Buddha*

30."Tomorrow is often the busiest day of the week." — *Spanish Proverb*

31."The key is not to prioritize what's on your schedule but to schedule your priorities." — *Stephen Covey*

32."Your time is limited, so don't waste it living someone else's life." — *Steve Jobs*

33."It's not enough to be busy; so are the ants. The question is: what are we busy about?" — *Henry David Thoreau*

34."The future depends on what you do today." — *Mahatma Gandhi*

35."Time is the scarcest resource and unless it is managed, nothing else can be managed." — *Peter Drucker*

36."Time is the longest distance between two places." — *Tennessee Williams*

37."The only way to do great work is to love what you do." — ***Steve Jobs***

38."The more you know yourself, the more you value your time." — ***Maxime Lagacé***

39."The key is in not spending time, but in investing it." — ***Stephen R. Covey***

40."The best way to predict the future is to create it." — ***Peter Drucker***

41."The essence of self—discipline is to do the important thing rather than the urgent thing." — ***Barry Werner***

42. "Your time is your life. That is why the greatest gift you can give someone is your time." — *Rick Warren*

43. "Success is not in what you have, but who you are." — *Bo Bennett*

44. "Time management is really life management." — *Brian Tracy*

45. "It's not the daily increase but daily decrease. Hack away at the unessential." — *Bruce Lee*

46. "The more you try to do, the less you actually accomplish." — *Ron Kaufman*

47. "The more you do, the more you have to do." — ***Dilip Bathija***

48. "Don't say you don't have enough time. You have exactly the same number of hours per day that were given to Helen Keller, Pasteur, Michelangelo, Mother Teresa, Leonardo da Vinci, Thomas Jefferson, and Albert Einstein." — ***H. Jackson Brown Jr.***

49. "When you kill time, remember that it has no resurrection." — ***A.W. Tozer***

50. "The greatest amount of wasted time is the time not getting started." — ***Dawson Trotman***

51."Time is the most valuable thing a man can spend." – *Theophrastus*

52."Time is what prevents everything from happening at once." — *John Archibald Wheeler*

53."Time is a created thing. Say 'yes' to it." — *Miles Davis*

54."Time is the coin of your life. It is the only coin you have, and only you can determine how it will be spent. Be careful lest you let other people spend it for you." — *Carl Sandburg*

55."One can find time for everything if one is never in a hurry." — *Mikhail Bulgakov*

56."The key is not to prioritize what's on your schedule but to schedule your priorities." — ***Stephen Covey***

57."The future depends on what you do today." — ***Mahatma Gandhi***

58."Time is the scarcest resource and unless it is managed, nothing else can be managed." — ***Peter Drucker***

59."Time is more valuable than money. You can get more money, but you cannot get more time." — ***Jim Rohn***

60."The essence of self—discipline is to do the important thing rather than the urgent thing." — ***Barry Werner***

61. "Your time is your life. That is why the greatest gift you can give someone is your time." — **_Rick Warren_**

62. "Success is not in what you have, but who you are." — **_Bo Bennett_**

63. "Time management is really life management." — **_Brian Tracy_**

64. "It's not the daily increase but daily decrease. Hack away at the unessential." — **_Bruce Lee_**

65. "The best time to plant a tree was 20 years ago. The second best time is now." — **_Chinese Proverb_**

66."The more you try to do, the less you actually accomplish." — ***Ron Kaufman***

67."The more you do, the more you have to do." — ***Dilip Bathija***

68."You can't make up for lost time. You can only do better in the future." — ***Ashley Ormon***

69."Don't say you don't have enough time. You have exactly the same number of hours per day that were given to Helen Keller, Pasteur, Michelangelo, Mother Teresa, Leonardo da Vinci, Thomas Jefferson, and Albert Einstein." — ***H. Jackson Brown Jr.***

70."When you kill time, remember that it has no resurrection." — *A.W. Tozer*

71."The greatest amount of wasted time is the time not getting started." — *Dawson Trotman*

72."Time is what prevents everything from happening at once." — **John Archibald Wheeler**

73."To achieve great things, two things are needed: a plan and not quite enough time." — **Leonard Bernstein**

74."Time is a created thing. Say 'yes' to it." — **Miles Davis**

75."Time is the coin of your life. It is the only coin you have, and only you can determine how it will be spent. Be careful lest you let other people spend it for you." — **Carl Sandburg**

76."One can find time for everything if one is never in a hurry." — *Mikhail Bulgakov*

77."Your time is limited, so don't waste it living someone else's life." — *Steve Jobs*

78."The future depends on what you do today." — *Mahatma Gandhi*

79."Time is the scarcest resource and unless it is managed, nothing else can be managed." — **Peter Drucker**

80."The essence of self—discipline is to do the important thing rather than the urgent thing." — *Barry Werner*

81."Your time is your life. That is why the greatest gift you can give someone is your time." — *Rick Warren*

82."Success is not in what you have, but who you are." — *Bo Bennett*

83."Time management is really life management." — *Brian Tracy*

84."It's not the daily increase but daily decrease. Hack away at the unessential." — *Bruce Lee*

85."The more you try to do, the less you actually accomplish." — *Ron Kaufman*

86."The more you do, the more you have to do." — *Dilip Bathija*

87."You can't make up for lost time. You can only do better in the future." — *Ashley Ormon*

88."Don't say you don't have enough time. You have exactly the same number of hours per day that were given to Helen Keller, Pasteur, Michelangelo, Mother

Teresa, Leonardo da Vinci, Thomas Jefferson, and Albert Einstein." — ***H. Jackson Brown Jr.***

89."When you kill time, remember that it has no resurrection." — ***A.W. Tozer***

90."The greatest amount of wasted time is the time not getting started." — ***Dawson Trotman***

91."Time is the most valuable thing a man can spend." – ***Theophrastus***

92."Time is what prevents everything from happening at once." — ***John Archibald Wheeler***

93. "Time is a created thing. Say 'yes' to it." — *Miles Davis*

94. "Time is the coin of your life. It is the only coin you have, and only you can determine how it will be spent. Be careful lest you let other people spend it for you." — *Carl Sandburg*

95. "One can find time for everything if one is never in a hurry." — *Mikhail Bulgakov*

96. "The key is not to prioritize what's on your schedule but to schedule your priorities." — *Stephen Covey*

97. "The future depends on what you do today." — *Mahatma Gandhi*

98."Time is the scarcest resource and unless it is managed, nothing else can be managed." — *Peter Drucker*

99."Time is the school in which we learn, time is the fire in which we burn." — *Delmore Schwartz*

100."Mastering time management is mastering life's flow." — **Tony Robbins**

101."Time is the currency of life; spend it wisely." — **Debasish Mridha**

102."The time you enjoy wasting is not wasted time." — **Bertrand Russell**

103."You cannot turn back the clock, but you can wind it up again." — **Bonnie Prudden**

104."Time slips away like grains of sand never to return again." – *Robin Sharma*

105."Time is free, but it's priceless. You can't own it, but you can use it. You can't keep it, but you can spend it. Once you've lost it you can never get it back." – *Harvey Mackay*

Time Management Quotations From Unknown

Figures

1.Time is the most valuable asset we possess; invest it wisely."

2."The key to success is not just working hard, but working smart with your time."

3."Don't waste time on things that don't matter; focus on what does."

4."Time management is the bridge between dreams and accomplishments."

5."Those who make the best use of their time make the best of their lives."

6."Time is an equal opportunity resource; it's how we use it that makes the difference."

7."Procrastination steals time; conquer it before it conquers you."

8."Time is the canvas of productivity; paint it with purpose."

9."Time is a river; you can either go with the flow or steer your own course."

10."Time management is about managing your choices, not just your time."

11."A minute wasted is an opportunity lost."

12."The best time to start managing your time was yesterday; the second best is now."

13."The clock never stops ticking; use every tick wisely."

14."To achieve greatness, respect the time it takes to get there."

15."Efficiency is the road to success paved with time management."

16."Time is limited, but possibilities are endless."

17."Focus on what's important now, and you won't regret later."

18."Time wasted on regrets is time lost on possibilities."

19."Tomorrow's success is built on today's time management."

20."Don't let time manage you; manage your time."

21."Time management is the best gift you can give yourself."

22."Success leaves footprints in the sands of time."

23. "Use time as a tool, not as a crutch."

24. "Tame your time, and you'll master your destiny."

25. "Time management is the art of balancing moments."

26. "Your life's story is written with the ink of time."

27. "Time is like a camera; focus on what's essential and capture the moments that matter."

28. "Make time for what sets your soul on fire."

29. "The magic of time management is in the moments it creates."

30."Time management is the dance between discipline and freedom."

31."Don't wait for the perfect time; create it."

32."The master of time management is the master of their fate."

33."The more time you spend on something, the more it becomes a part of who you are."

34."Time management is self-management."

35."Don't just dream; take control of your time and make it a reality."

36."Time is the canvas; your actions are the brushstrokes."

37."Time management is a habit; build it into your life."

38."The value of time is realized in its scarcity."

39."Use time wisely, for it cannot be borrowed or saved for later."

40."The clock is always ticking, but the choice is yours on how you respond."

41."You cannot manage time; you can only manage yourself within time."

42."Make the most of now, for it is the only moment guaranteed."

43."Time management is the foundation of achievement."

44."Time is a non-renewable resource; use it wisely."

45."The true value of time is measured by the memories it creates."

46."Time is like money; it's essential to budget it wisely."

47."Time management is the compass that guides you to your destination."

48. "Every second counts; treat them as precious gems."

49. "Time management is about doing the right things at the right time."

50. "Time lost is a dream deferred."

51. "Time is a treasure; spend it wisely, and it multiplies."

52. "Tomorrow's success depends on today's time management."

53. "Time is the thread that weaves the fabric of our lives."

54."Time management is the master key to unlock your potential."

55."The clock never stops; cherish the moments while they last."

56."Time is the most significant equalizer; everyone has the same 24 hours."

57."Time management is a journey, not a destination."

58."Time is the canvas of opportunity; paint it with action."

59."The more you value time, the more time you'll have to value."

60."Time management is the art of balancing work and play."

61."Time is the raw material of creation; make something beautiful out of it."

62."One cannot buy, rent, or barter more time; use what you have wisely."

63."Time management is the key to unlocking productivity's door."

64."Time is like a river; you can either sail with its flow or swim against it."

65."Time is an asset; invest it in endeavors that appreciate."

66."Time is the most valuable resource because it is limited."

67."Don't be a prisoner of time; be its master."

68."The secret to time management is prioritizing what matters most."

69."Time is the currency of productivity; spend it on high-value tasks."

70."Time management is the heartbeat of efficiency."

71."Time is a gift; open it with purpose."

72."Time management is the blueprint of success."

73."Time is a fleeting companion; embrace it before it's gone."

74."The clock is the referee of life; use its ticks wisely."

75."Time is a healer, but it is also a revealer."

76."Time management is the bridge between mediocrity and greatness."

77."Don't chase time; create moments that last a lifetime."

78."Time is the sculptor; your actions are the clay."

79."Time is constant; it's our choices that vary."

80."Time management is the compass that points toward purpose."

81."Make time for the people and activities that bring you joy."

82."Time is the canvas of creativity; paint your masterpiece."

83."The clock is a silent teacher; listen to its lessons."

84."Time management is the harmony of work and leisure."

85."Time is a teacher that reveals life's lessons."

86."Time management is not about doing more; it's about doing what matters most."

87."Time management is an art, and it requires practice and patience to master."

88."Time management is not about doing more; it's about doing what matters most."

89."Time management is an art, and it requires practice and patience to master."

90."Time management is an art, and it requires practice and patience to master."

91."Time management is not about doing more; it's about doing what matters most."

92."Time management is an art, and it requires practice and patience to master."

93."Time management is not about doing more; it's about doing what matters most."

CHAPTER 2

SUBSTANCIAL QUOTES ABOUT

PROCRASTINATION

1."A pursuit for perfection is the most leading cause of procrastination." —*Neeraj Agnihotri*

2."The momentum of continuous action fuels motivation, while procrastination kills motivation." —*Steve Pavlina*

3."Procrastinate now and panic later." —*Anonymous*

4."Procrastination is the thief of time." — *Edward Young*

5. "The greatest amount of wasted time is the time not getting started." *—Anonymous*

6."You don't have to see the whole staircase, just take the first step." *—Martin Luther King, jr.*

7."Procrastination does nothing more than add to do your list. Do it, be done with it." *—Catherine Pulsifer*

8."Doubt increases with inaction. Clarity reveals itself in momentum. Growth comes from progress. For all these reasons, begin."*— Brandon Burchard*

9."Following things is the only thing that separates dreamers from people that accomplish great things."*—*

Gene Hayden

10."Waiting is a trap. There will always be a reason to wait. The truth is there are only two things in life, reason, and result, and reasons simply don't count."— ***Robert Anthony***

11."Procrastination is the grave in which opportunity is buried."—***Anonymous***

12."Don't procrastinate, life is too short. Do things as they come to you, live your life like a high-speed sports."—***Julie Hebert***

13."Concentrate all your thoughts upon the work in hand. The sun's rays do not burn until brought to a focus."

—***Alexander Graham Bell***

14."The problem with tomorrow is that I have never seen tomorrow. Tomorrow doesn't exist. Tomorrow only exists in the mind of dreamers and losers." — ***Robert Kiyosaki***

16."Getting an idea should be like sitting on a pin; it should make you jump up and do something." — ***E.L. Simpson***

17."Nothing is less productive than to make more efficient what should not be done at all."—***Peter Drucker***

18."It is not because things are difficult that we do not dare, it is because we do not dare that they are difficult."—***Seneca***

19."Procrastination is like a credit card, it's a lot of fun until you get the bill."—*Anonymous*

20."A man who procrastinates in his choosing will inevitably have his choice made for him."—*Hunter s Thompson*

21."Procrastination makes easy things hard, hard things harder."—*Anonymous*

22."Begin while others are procrastinating. Work while others are wishing." —*William Arthur Ward*

23."Procrastination is the foundation of all disasters."—

Pandora Poikilos

24."Delay negates purpose, procrastination adds pressure."— ***Martin Uzochukwu Ugwu***

25."The breeding ground of fear is procrastination and inaction. We overcome them not by preparation but by taking action."— ***Debashish Mridha***

26."The secret of getting ahead is getting started."—

Anonymous

27."Stop putting it off! Procrastination breeds guilt, guilt breeds depression, and depression breeds failure."—

Barbara Corcoran

28. "Even if you are on the right track, you will get run over if you just sit there."— *Arthur Godfrey*

29. "The only difference between failure and success is the ability to take action."—*Alexander Graham Bell*

30. "Stop getting afraid of what you can do wrong and start getting excited about what you can do right."—

Anonymous

31. "The most effective way to do is to do it."—*Amelia Earhart*

32. "Putting off an easy task makes it hard and putting off a hard task makes it impossible."— *George h Lorimer*

33."The dread of doing a task uses up more time and energy than doing the task itself."—*Rita Emmett*

34."Do something instead of killing time. Because time is killing you."—*Paulo Coelho*

35."Once I finished, I got that procrastination monkey off my back and I started seeing doors opening."—*Eric Thomas*

36."We are so scared of being judged that we look for every excuse to procrastinate."—*Erica Jong*

37."Remember action today can prevent a crisis tomorrow."— *Steve Shallenberger*

38."The scary thing is the more I slack off the more it piles up and the more it piles up, the more I slack off."— *Amelia Mysko*

39."Sometimes the best way of going ahead with life is doing what is necessary, instead of procrastinating. Often a joyful patch is just a few hours away."— *Kunal Jain*

40."When there is a hill to climb don't think that waiting will make it smaller."— *Anonymous*

41."I'd be more frightened by not using whatever abilities I'd been given. I'd be more frightened by procrastination and laziness."—*Denzel Washington*

42."The man who waits to know everything is the man who never does anything."— *Craig D Lounsbrough*

43."Procrastination is the lazy cousin of fear. When we feel anxiety about an activity, we postpone it."—*Noelle Hancock*

44."A day can really slip when you're deliberately avoiding what you are supposed to do."— *Bill Watterson*

45."If you want to get ahead in life, I've found that the most useless word is tomorrow."— *Jose N Harris*

46."In delay there lies no plenty."—*William Shakespeare*

47. "Do first what you don't want to do most."—*Clifford Cohen*

48. "Those who work their land will have abundant food, but those who chase fantasies have no sense."– *The bible (Proverbs 12:11)*

49. "How to stop procrastination starts with believing that you can overcome procrastination."—*Robert Moment*

50. "What is deferred is not avoided."—*Thomas More*

51. "You may not be punished for your procrastination, but sure you will be punished by your procrastination."—*Debashish Mridha*

52."Things may come to those who wait, but only the things left by those who hustle."—*Abraham Lincoln*

53."If you wait until the wind and the weather are just right, you'll never plant anything and never harvest anything."— *The bible (Ecclesiastes 1:14)*

54."How soon not now becomes never."— *Martin Luther*

55."Someday is not a day of the week."— *Janet Dailey*

56."Don't wait the time will never be right."— *Napoleon Hill*

57."My advice is never to do tomorrow what you can do today. Procrastination is the thief of time."—*Charles Dickens*

58."Procrastination is opportunity's natural assassin.—*Victor Kiam*

59."A year from now you wish you had started today."—*Karen lamb*

60."If we wait until we've satisfied all the uncertainties, it may be too late."— *Lee Iocca*

61."What may be done at any time may be done at no time."—*Scottish proverb*

62."Tomorrow is often the busiest day of the week."—

Spanish proverb

63."The worst kind of procrastination is reading a

procrastination quote, feeling guilt, and not doing

anything about it."— *Unknown*

64."How does a project get to be a year behind schedule?

One day at a time."— *Fred Brooks*

65."Neither a wise nor a brave man lies down on the

track of history to wait for the train of the future to run

over him." *—Dwight d Eisenhower*

66."He who thinks much on every step he takes will

always stay on one leg." — *Chinese proverb*

67."Yesterday is a canceled check, tomorrow is a promissory note; today is the only cash you have, so spend it wisely."— ***Kim Lyons***

68."The least productive people are usually the ones who are most in favor of holding meetings."—***Thomas Sowell***

69."Often greater risk is involved in postponement than in making a wrong decision."—***Harry A. Hopf***

70."There is nothing so fatal to character as half—finished tasks."—***David Lloyd George***

71."You can't get much done in life if you only work on the days when you feel good." —***Jerry West***

72."Procrastination is, hands down, our favorite form of self-sabotage." —*Alyce P. Cornyn*

73."Doing things at the last minute reminds us of the importance of doing things in the first minute."—*Matshona Dhliwayo*

74."Motivation is what gets you started. Habit is what keeps you going."—*Jim Rohn*

75."There are only so many tomorrows."—*Michael Landon*

76."My biggest regret could be summed up in one word, and that's procrastination."—**Ron Cooper**

77."When it comes to procrastination and overthinking, we have to overcome our self-doubt." — *Jay Shetty*

78."Begin doing what you want to do now. We are not living in eternity. We have only this moment, sparkling like a star in our hand—and melting like a snowflake.
— Francis Bacon

79."In a moment of decision, the best thing you can do is the right thing to do, the next best thing is the wrong thing, and the worst thing you can do is nothing." —
Theodore Roosevelt

80. "If you have goals and procrastination you have nothing. If you have goals, and you take action, you will have anything you want."— *Thomas J. Vilord*

81. "All hard work brings a profit, but mere talk leads only to poverty." —*The bible (Proverbs 14:23)*

82. "If you procrastinate when faced with a big difficult problem… break the problem into parts, and handle one part at a time." — *Robert Collier*

83. "Never put off till tomorrow the book you can read today." —*Holbrook Jackson*

84. "Action will destroy your procrastination." —*Og Mandino*

85. "Diligent hands will rule, but laziness ends in forced labor." — *Anonymous*

86. "Procrastination is a dream slayer, slavemaker, and life taker that shadows your mind and obscure your goals. Action is a superpower, take it." — *Leaura Alderson*

87. "Procrastination is one of the most common and deadliest diseases and its toll on happiness and success is heavy." —*Wayne Gretzky*

88. "Today stop making excuses why you can't get it done and start focusing on all the reasons why you must make it happen." — *Anonymous*

89. "Continuous improvement is better than delayed perfection." —*Mark Twain*

90. "You may delay, but time will not." —*Benjamin Franklin*

91. "You cannot escape the responsibility of tomorrow by evading it today." — *Abraham Lincoln*

92. "If you want to make an easy job seem mighty hard, just keep putting off doing it." – *Olin Miller*

93. "Procrastination is the thief of time, collar him." – *Charles Dickens*

94."Procrastination is not Laziness", I tell him. "It is fear. Call it by its right name, and forgive yourself." – *Julia Cameron*

95."The greatest amount of wasted time is the not getting started." – *Dawson Trotman*

96."If you love life, don't waste time, for time is what life is made up of." – *Bruce Lee*

CHAPTER 3

SUBSTANCIAL QUOTES ABOUT LAZINZESS

1.“Laziness is a luxurious mindset that I cannot afford to own.” – *Nakia R. Laushaul*

2. “If you wait for the mango fruits to fall, you'd be wasting your time while others are learning how to climb the tree.” – *Michael Bassey Johnson*

3. “Laziness is a habit which makes you fall in the pit, lazy people don't act but prefer to sit, they delay action with some excuse, laziness is of no use.” – *Ron Sen*

4. "We may regard certain days as free days. Free days are however fee days. We will pay later." – ***Ernest Agyemang Yeboah***

5."If you ask me which the real hereditary sin of human nature is, do you imagine I shall answer pride, or luxury, or ambition, or egotism? No; I shall say indolence. Who conquers indolence will conquer all the rest. Indeed all good principles must stagnate without mental activity." – ***Johann Zimmerman***

6."Pessimism is a primary source of passivity." –

Barbara W. Tuchman

7."With work misery is relieved, with laziness misery is multiplied." – *Abhijit Naskar*

8. "One excuse, could destroy a multitude of chances." – *Anthony Liccione*

9. "Laziness demands misery." – *Bryant McGill*

10."Try making a good attempt not a good excuse." — *Amit Kalantri*

11."Where there is less pain, there is also less pay." –

Auliq Ice

12."I was trained to turn loneliness into laziness." – *Bill*

Callahan

13. "Laziness is a devastating disease." – *K.P. Kelly*

14. "Laziness is always your fault. It is the sign that a

man has persevered in uselessness for too long." – *Idries*

Shah

15."Laziness is a secret ingredient that goes into failure. But it's only kept a secret from the person who fails." — *Robert Half*

16."In doing nothing men learn to do evil." – *Marcus Porcius Cato*

17. "The devil often finds work for them who find none for themselves." – *Benjamin Whichcote*

18."The generality of mankind is lazy. What distinguishes men of genuine achievement from the rest of us is not so much their intellectual powers and aptitudes as their curiosity, their energy, their fullest use of their potentialities. Nobody really knows how smart or talented he is until he finds the incentives to use himself to the fullest." – *Sydney J. Harris*

19. "A year from now you may wish you had started today." – *Karen Lamb*

20. "Diligence is the mother of good fortune, and the goal of a good intention was never reached through its opposite, laziness." – *Miguel de Cervantes*

21. "Inspiration is a guest that does not willingly visit the lazy." – *Tchaikovsky*

22. "Idleness is the Dead Sea that swallows all virtues." – *Benjamin Franklin*

23."Folks who never do any more than they get paid for, never get paid for any more than they do." – *Elbert Hubbard*

24. "Of all the cankers of human happiness, none corrodes it with so silent, yet so baneful, a tooth, as indolence." — *Thomas Jefferson*

25. "Kill the darlings in your life. Laziness, wishful thinking, procrastination; kill them." – *Bangambiki Habyarimana*

26. "Indolence is a delightful but distressing state. We must be doing something to be happy." – *William Hazlitt*

27. "It is easier to move from failure to success than from excuses to success."

— *John C. Maxwell*

28. "Luck is always the last refuge of laziness and incompetence." – *James Cash Penney*

29."Idle hands are the devil's playthings." – ***Benjamin***

Franklin

30."Luck never brings luxury to the lazy." – ***Amit***

Kalantri

31. "There is a great volcano sleeping in every laziness!"
– ***Mehmet Murat ildan***

32. "The only time a lazy man ever succeeds is when he

tries to do nothing." – ***Evan Esar***

33."Lazy people fact: #2347827309018287.You were too

lazy to read this number." – ***Skylar Blue***

34. "The world is full of willing people; some willing to work, the rest willing to let them." – **Robert Frost**

35."Reclined legs don't get fed, they get limp like boiled spaghetti. Walk it out!" – **T.F. Hodge**

36. "Some folks can look so busy doing nothing that they seem indispensable." – **Kim Hubbard**

"Too many people itch for what they want without scratching for it." – **Thomas Taylor**

37. "Laziness is nothing more than the habit of resting before you get tired." – *Jules Renard*

38. "The path of least resistance makes all rivers, and some men, crooked." – *Napolean Hill*

39. "Laziness grows on people; it begins in cobwebs and ends in iron chains." – *Sir Thomas Fowell Buxton*

40. "Obsessed is a word the lazy use to describe the dedicated." – *Unknown*

41. "Stop sleeping, Get to work! You will have much time to sleep when you die." – ***Michael Bassey Johnson***

42. "We wake up to be alive and to revive our lives; we don't wake up to keep sleeping! We wake up not just to be alive, but also to keep our works alive and mind the business of the day! When you wake up, revive your work!" – ***Ernest Agyemang Yeboah***

43. "I can't relate to lazy people. We don't speak the same language. I don't understand you; I don't want to understand you." – ***Kobe Bryant***

44. "Success is not an easy thing! Success is allergic to laziness! However, it is amenable to intelligence and diligence." – ***Enock Maregesi***

45. "Make it your aim today to be a "champion" in the making. You are not going to be hoisted up on the podium this afternoon, but inch by inch, small but meaningful decision multiplied will get you to where you want to be and beyond. Don't you dare despise small beginnings." – ***Chris J. Gregas***

46. "I'd be more frightened by not using whatever abilities I'd been given. I'd be more frightened by procrastination and laziness." – ***Denzel Washington***

47. "When you are willing to replace mundane excuses with hard work and your laziness with determination, nothing can prevent you from succeeding." – *Dr Prem Jagyasi*

48. "Uncomplicate it. Don't make excuses. Some of life's biggest heartaches come from missed opportunities and lame excuses. Don't miss out on what could be the best chapter in your life because you're too busy rereading the last one.— *Kandi Steiner*

49. "You can have the results you want, or you can have excuses. You can't have both." – ***Clyde Lee Dennis***

50. "Laziness is the one common deficiency in mankind that blocks the establishment of a perfect world in which everyone leads a happy life." – ***William Feather***

51. "If you are going to quit anything, quit being lazy, quit making excuses and quit waiting for the right time."

– ***Unknown***

52. "It is the man who has hammered his laziness out of the stubborn material of life for whom we chant praise and halleluiah." – ***Christopher Morley***

53."But your laziness leads you astray; your greed makes you dumb; your gluttony makes enemies for you." – ***Miriam Lichtheim***

54. "Laziness is when you accede to the misconception that work is unnecessary." – ***Innocent Mwatsikesimbe***

55."Sloth makes all things difficult, but industry all easy; and he that riseth late must trot all day, and shall scarce overtake his business at night; while laziness travels so slowly, that poverty soon overtakes him." – *Benjamin Franklin*

56. "Laziness erodes a person of his enthusiasm and energy. As a result the person loses all opportunities and finally becomes dejected and frustrated. The worst thing is that he stops believing in himself." – *Sam Veda*

57. "People who are in the habit of enjoying the comfort of inaction often pay a high price in the end." – *Dr. T.P. Chia*

58. "Lazy begets poverty every time!" – *Mark Dawson*

59."One must avoid that wicked temptress, Laziness." –

Horace

CONCLUSION

" The really happy people are those who have broken the chains of procrastination, those who find satisfaction in doing the job at hand. They're full of eagerness, zest, and productivity. You can be, too." – **Norman Vincent Peale**

It takes discipline, perseverance and determination to put into practice the principles you've discovered in this book. But also remember that every little step counts. Every day, every hour, every minute you use productively brings you a little closer to your goals. Your time is your life, it is the seed of your destiny, manage it wisely. Our entire life depends on it. On this note, I wish you every success in your journey towards better time management.